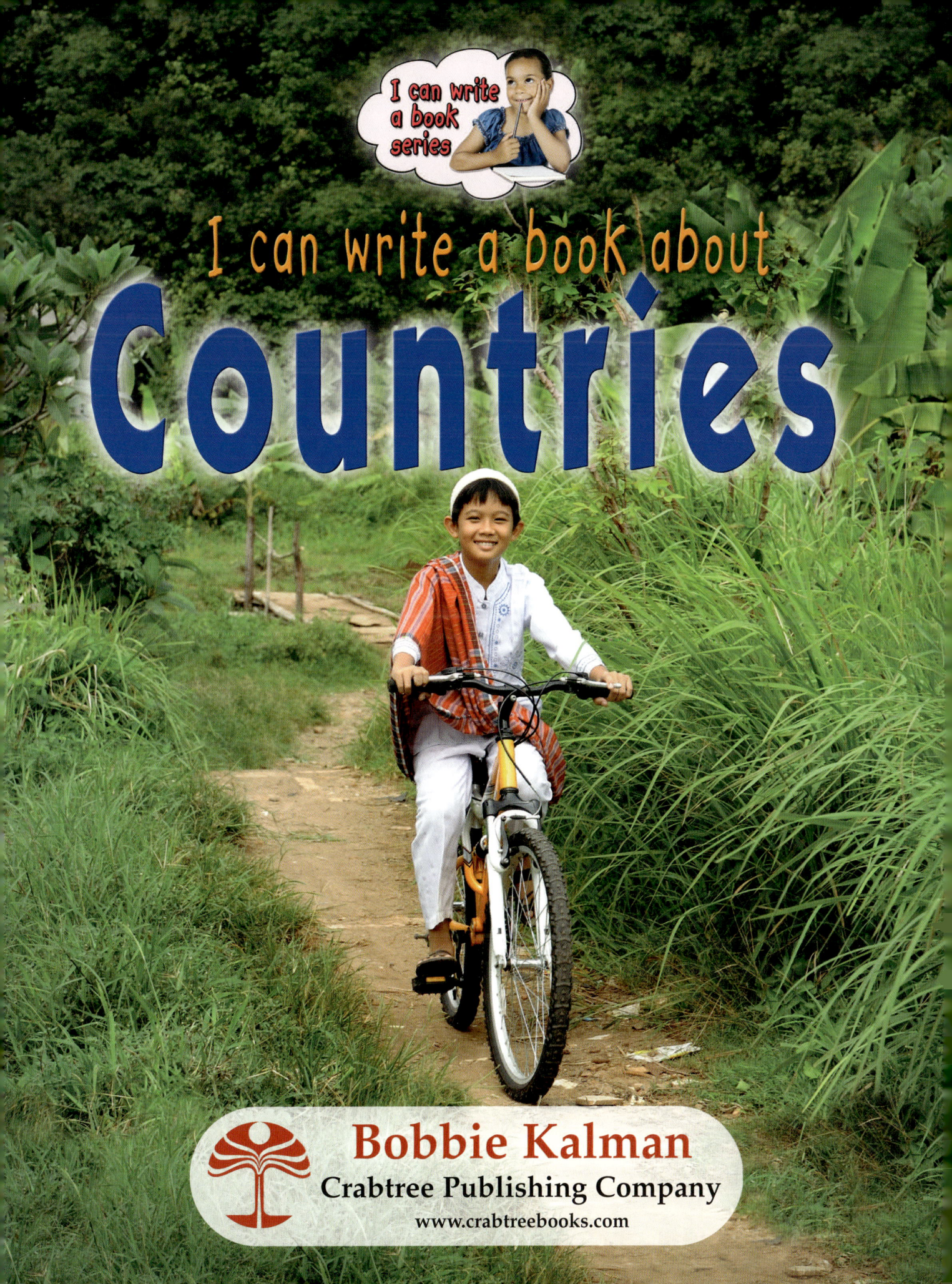

Created by Bobbie Kalman

For our good friends Scott and Ruth Aspinall,
who travel the world and treat us to the best international cuisine
at their home and restaurant, the Epicurean

Author and Editor-in-Chief
Bobbie Kalman

Editors
Kathy Middleton
Crystal Sikkens

Photo research
Bobbie Kalman

Design
Bobbie Kalman
Katherine Berti
Samantha Crabtree
(logo and cover)

Prepress technician
Katherine Berti

Print and production coordinator
Katherine Berti

Illustrations
Scott Mooney: p. 11 (top right)
Bonna Rouse: p. 9 (ballot box), 11 (top left)
Margaret Amy Salter: p. 8 (snowflakes)

Photographs
Adobe/Image Club: p. 10 (indigenous people)
Bobbie Kalman: back cover inset, p. 5 (top right), p. 22 (bottom left inset)
Expressive Maps/Katherine Berti: p. 12 (bottom)
Istockphoto: p. 26 (bottom)
Shutterstock: cover, logo, title page, p. 3, 4, 5 (bottom), 7, 8, 9 (top left, top right, Earth, bottom center, bottom right [all except workshop]), 10 (all except indigenous people), 11, 12 (top), 13, 14, 15, 16, 17 (all except top left, people of Indonesia), 18, 19, 20, 21, 22 (all except bottom left inset), 23, 24, 25, 26 (top), 27, 28, 29, 30 (all except bottom right inset); Chen WS: p. 17 (top left, people of Indonesia); Jacek Kadaj: p. 30 (bottom right inset); Jeff Schultes: p. 9 (bottom right [workshop inset])
PhotoDisk: p. 9 (apples)

Library and Archives Canada Cataloguing in Publication

Kalman, Bobbie
    I can write a book about countries / Bobbie Kalman.

(I can write a book series)
Includes index.
Issued also in electronic format.
ISBN 978-0-7787-7988-9 (bound).--ISBN 978-0-7787-7997-1 (pbk.)

    1. Geography--Authorship--Juvenile literature. 2. Composition
(Language arts)--Juvenile literature. 3. English language--Composition
and exercises--Juvenile literature. 4. Book design--Juvenile literature.
I. Title. II. Series: Kalman, Bobbie. I can write a book.

G133.K344 2012   j910'.02   C2012-901154-1

Library of Congress Cataloging-in-Publication Data

Kalman, Bobbie.
  I can write a book about countries / Bobbie Kalman.
       p. cm. -- (I can write a book series)
  Includes index.
  ISBN 978-0-7787-7988-9 (reinforced library binding : alk. paper) -- ISBN 978-0-7787-7997-1 (pbk. : alk. paper) -- ISBN 978-1-4271-7879-4 (electronic pdf) -- ISBN 978-1-4271-7994-4 (electronic html)
 1. Geography--Juvenile literature. 2. Map reading--Juvenile literature. I. Title.

G133.K2535 2012
808.06'691--dc23
                                                           2012005752

Crabtree Publishing Company

www.crabtreebooks.com   1-800-387-7650

Printed in Canada/042012/KR20120316

Copyright © **2012 CRABTREE PUBLISHING COMPANY**. All rights reserved. No part of this publication may be reproduced, stored in a retrieval system or be transmitted in any form or by any means, electronic, mechanical, photocopying, recording, or otherwise, without the prior written permission of Crabtree Publishing Company. In Canada: We acknowledge the financial support of the Government of Canada through the Canada Book Fund for our publishing activities.

Published in Canada
Crabtree Publishing
616 Welland Ave.
St. Catharines, Ontario
L2M 5V6

Published in the United States
Crabtree Publishing
PMB 59051
350 Fifth Avenue, 59th Floor
New York, New York 10118

Published in the United Kingdom
Crabtree Publishing
Maritime House
Basin Road North, Hove
BN41 1WR

Published in Australia
Crabtree Publishing
3 Charles Street
Coburg North
VIC 3058

Table of contents

A book about countries	4	Finding information	20
Parts of a book	6	Body of the book	22
Country words to know	8	Fonts or written words?	24
More country words	10	Revising and editing	26
Countries and continents	12	Designing your book	28
Where is the country?	14	Finishing up	29
Who lives there?	16	Cover and title page	30
Starting your book	18	Bobbie's country books	31
		Glossary and Index	32

A book about countries

Some books entertain us, and some teach us about our world. **Fiction** books are stories created from someone's imagination. **Non-fiction** books contain facts about animals, habitats, countries, landforms, or sports. They can also contain true stories about people. This non-fiction book shows you how to write and **publish** a non-fiction book about one or more **countries**. A country is an area of land with **borders**. A border is where one country ends and another begins. You can choose a country you are studying or one that you would love to visit. Perhaps your parents are from a country you would like to learn more about. Which country will you write about?

Writing a book about countries will help you discover the world!

Publishing your book will make you feel proud. To publish is to share the final copy of your work with others.

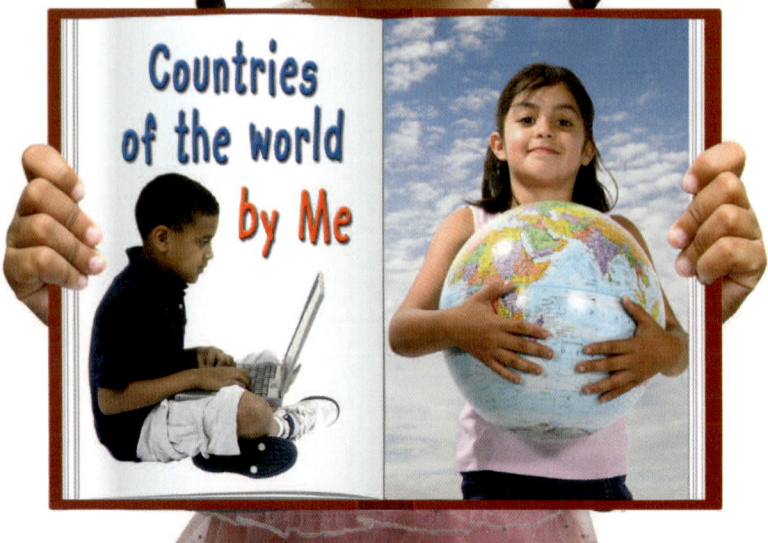

Meet Bobbie

My name is Bobbie Kalman. I am an **author** and a person who loves to travel. I was born in Hungary, lived in five countries, been a teacher in three, and traveled to dozens more. I love traveling because I see beautiful oceans and lands, meet wonderful people, enjoy other cultures, listen to great music, eat delicious foods, and learn different languages. Each time I write about a country, I find it so exciting that I want to travel there. You, too, will experience the joy of traveling when you write your own book about a country or countries. Not only will you be an author, you will also be a teacher when others read your book.

I loved teaching in the Bahamas and have visited my old school several times since then. I met this young student on one of my visits.

When others read your book, they will be learning from you. Besides being an author, you will be a teacher, too. This girl is pointing to Brazil on a map. Is her family from Brazil? Will she write about this country?

Parts of a book

You have probably written many reports in school. Writing a non-fiction book is like writing a report, but there are more parts to a book. There are also more pages. A book's pages are held together by a **cover**. A cover is the outside of the book. It is the first thing that people see. A good cover makes people want to read a book. The cover shown here is the cover of this book. Your cover will be different (see page 30). What will you put on the cover of your book about countries?

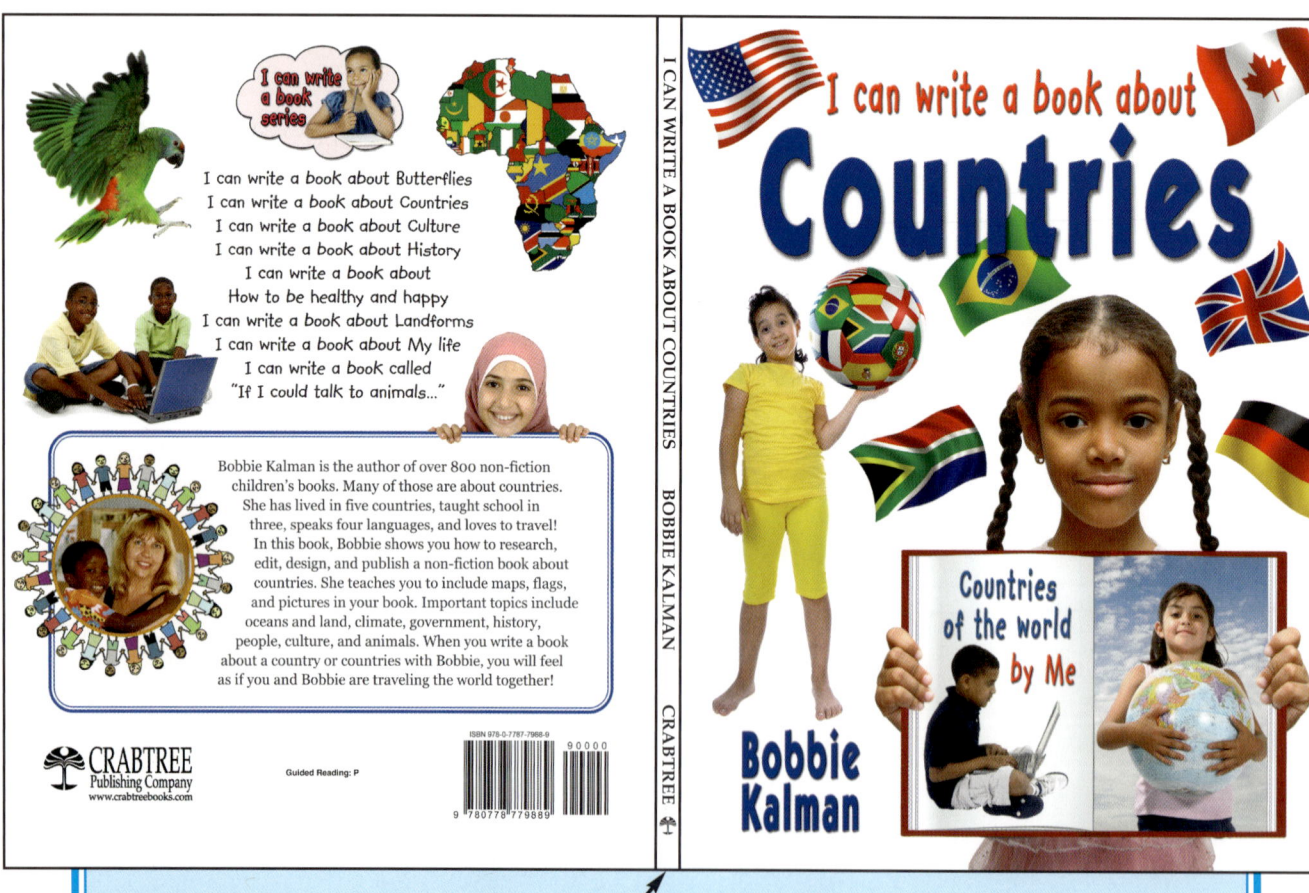

The back cover of the book may give you information about the author, **publisher**, price, and other books written by the author.

The **spine** separates the front and back covers. What information does it give you? How does it help you find the book on a bookshelf?

The front cover of the book contains the title of the book and the name of the author. It catches your attention with an interesting title and a great picture or pictures.

The title page

The first page inside the cover is the **title page**. The picture on the right shows the title page of this book. What information does it give you?

Copyright page

The second page in this book is the **copyright** page. Copyright means that people cannot copy all or parts of the book without the author's or publisher's permission. What else does it tell you? Turn to the copyright page in this book and find the following information:

- the names of the people who helped create this book
- the addresses of the publisher
- a **dedication**, or the words used to honor someone by placing his or her name in the book
- the **cataloging information**, a section of the page that tells the books's title, the name of the author, the year the book was published, and the type of book it is

Contents, glossary, index

The **table of contents** gives the names of the **chapters**, or sections, in the book and the page numbers on which they begin. The **glossary** is a small dictionary that explains special words used in the book. The **index** is an alphabetical list of the topics in the book with page numbers telling where those topics are covered.

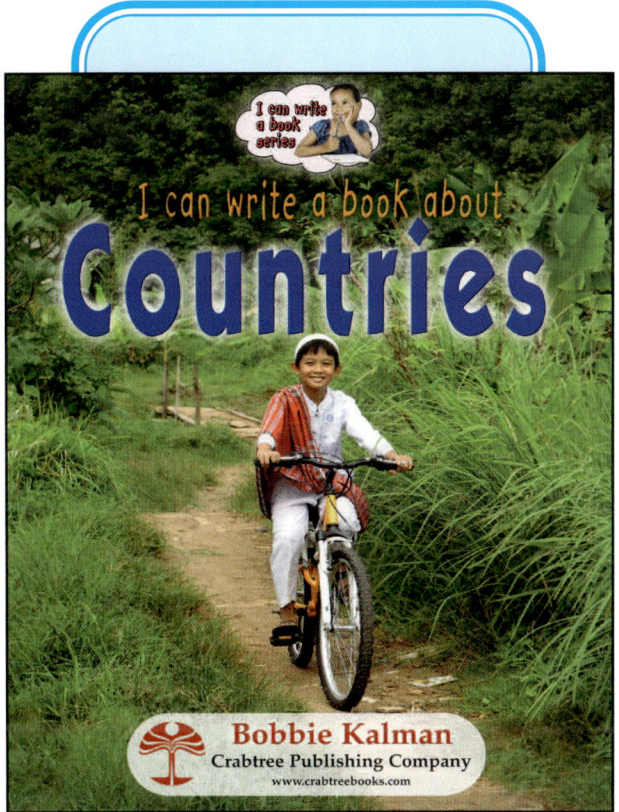

The top page shows the title page, and the bottom one shows the table of contents of this book.

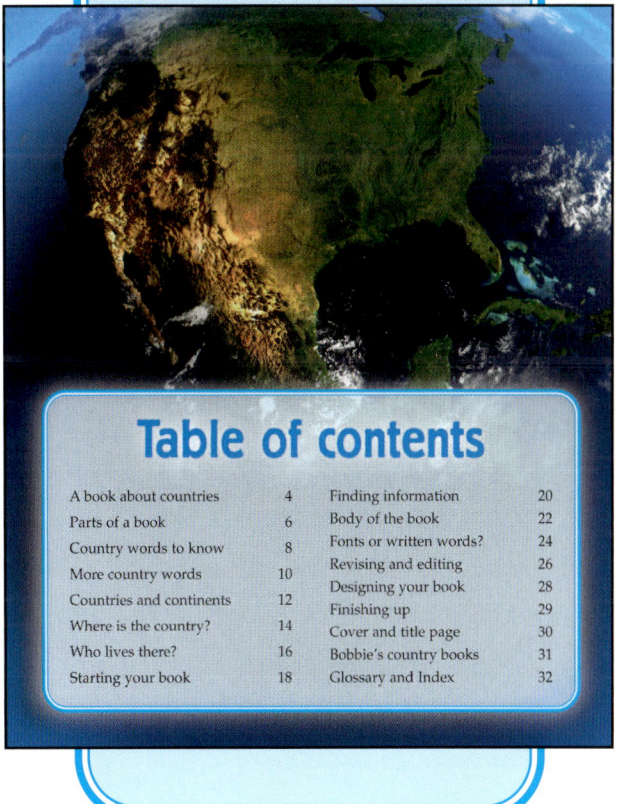

7

Country words to know

The next four pages introduce you to the most important words about countries. You will find information that will help you start writing your book. At the back of your own book, you could do a picture dictionary with definitions underneath, like the examples on these pages, or a word glossary like the one on page 32, or both, as on page 11.

An **archipelago** is a chain of **islands**. An island is an area of land with water all around it. This map shows the country of Japan, which is made up of a chain of islands.

A **border** is an imaginary line that separates countries or areas. This map shows Canada, the United States, Mexico, and some other countries. Each one is in a different color. The borders are where the colors change.

A **capital** is the city in which the **government** of a country is located. The capital of the United States is Washington, D.C. The **president** lives and works there in a building called the White House. The president is the head of the country.

Climate is the usual long-term weather in a country or area. Some countries have four seasons. Some have two. Which season is shown in this picture?

A **continent** is one of Earth's seven huge areas of land. Countries are part of continents.

Culture is how people live. It is the languages they speak, the clothes they wear, the foods they eat, the stories they tell, and the ways they celebrate. It is also the way they show their imagination through art, music, and writing.

Democracy is the type of government in which people **elect**, or choose their leaders, by voting in **elections**. A government rules a country or part of a country according to laws.

The **equator** is an imaginary line across the middle of Earth that divides the planet into two equal parts.

Farming is using land for growing fruits and vegetables and for raising animals for food.

History is stories, events, and ways of life from the past.

9

More country words

Indigenous, or native, people were the first people who lived in a country or area.

An **island** is land with water all around it. Some countries, such as Japan and Indonesia, are made up of many islands.

Landforms are the different shapes of land on Earth. Most countries have landforms such as caves, mountains, valleys, islands, volcanoes, cliffs, canyons, and more.

Language is how people communicate by talking or writing, using words they understand. Each country has one or more **official** languages. Official means approved by the government.

An **occupation** is someone's job or profession.

Population is the total number of people living in a country or area.

A **republic** is a country in which the people control the government through the **representatives** they have elected. A republic does not have a king or queen as the head of the country.

A **tropical** country is one that is near the equator and has a hot climate. Indonesia is a tropical country.

A **tsunami** is a giant sea wave created by an earthquake or a volcanic eruption under water. Tsunami waves can cause a lot of destruction on land. Countries such as Japan and Indonesia have been hit hard by tsunamis.

More definitions

desert A dry area with few plants, and very hot or cold temperatures

independence The state of being free from the rule of another country

prime minister The head of an elected government, such as the government of Canada

tradition The passing on of customs and beliefs from **generation** to generation

Countries and continents

Find Earth's continents on the map below. From biggest to smallest, they are Asia, Africa, North America, South America, Antarctica, Europe, and Australia/Oceania. The map also shows Earth's five oceans. From largest to smallest, the oceans are: Pacific, Atlantic, Indian, Southern, and Arctic. The equator is the dotted line across the middle of the map. It divides Earth into two sections—the **Northern Hemisphere** and **Southern Hemisphere**. When you write a book about a country, you need to show the country on a map, along with directions showing its location. The **compass rose** below left shows the directions on Earth: north, south, east, west. You can trace maps from an atlas or use a globe to draw your own.

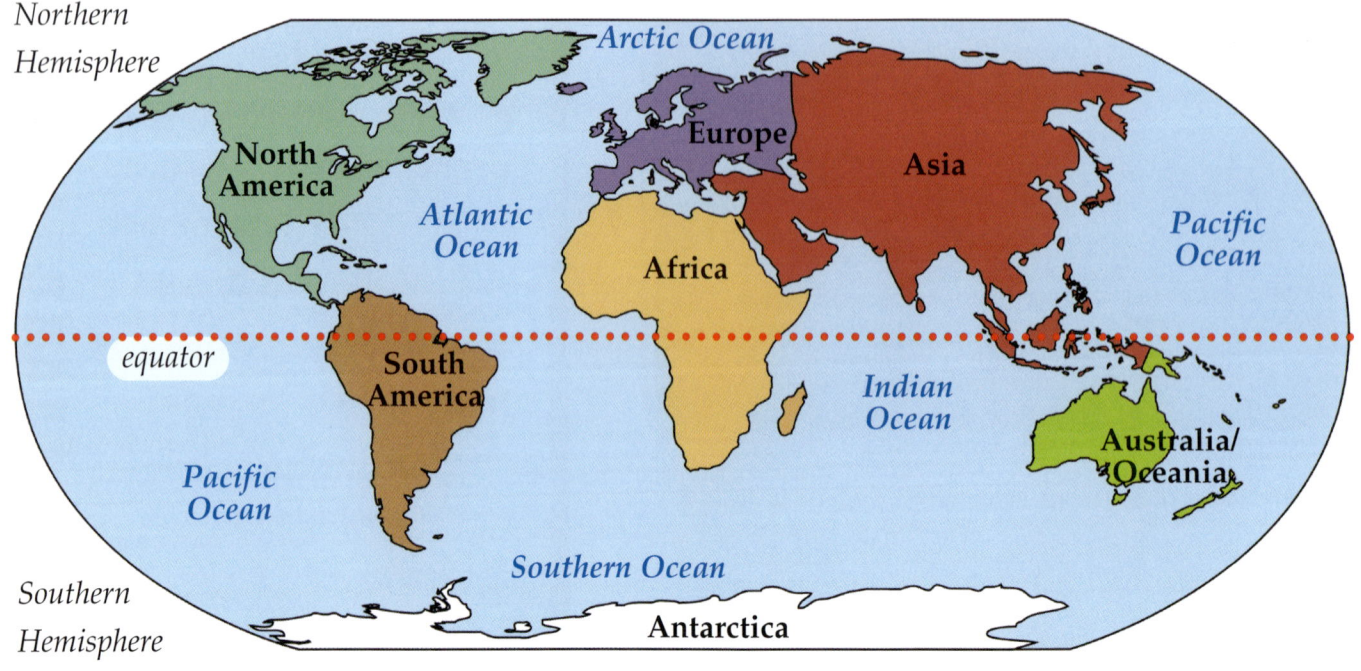

This map shows the countries of the world. You could trace or draw it to use in an ABC book or for a quiz about countries. The countries below are in alphabetical order. The first letter of each is on the map above. There are more countries starting with almost every letter. Which continent names start with the letter A? (See page 9.)

Write these country names in your notebook and find the countries on the map above. Which will you write about? Will you write an ABC book and include some of these countries?

Australia
Brazil
Canada
Denmark
Egypt
France
Germany
Hungary
India
Japan
Kenya
Libya
Mexico
New Zealand
Oman
Peru
Qatar
Russia
South Africa
Turkey
United States
Venezuela
Western Sahara
Yemen
Zambia

13

Where is the country?

Non-fiction books contain **big ideas**, or important topics. Big ideas about countries include location, climate, landforms, government, people, and culture. You could write a book about one country using these topics or talk about one big idea throughout several countries. The next four pages contain big ideas about countries that you may want to write about.

Is it near an ocean?

Countries are in different parts of the world. Some are far from oceans, and others are island chains called archipelagos, which are surrounded by oceans. Indonesia, Japan, and the Philippines are countries made up of many islands.

What kind of land?

Many countries, like Tibet and Peru, have very high mountains. Some, such as Indonesia, have dangerous volcanoes. What kind of landforms would you like to learn more about?

What is its climate?

Countries that are near the equator have a tropical climate. Some tropical countries, such as Brazil, have huge rain forests, where many animals live. Others, like Egypt, have hot, dry deserts. Countries that are far from the equator have four seasons: spring, summer, autumn, and winter.

Peru has high mountains.

capuchin monkey

Questions to ask myself
- On which continent is the country I am writing about?
- Is it close to an ocean?
- Is the country made up of islands?
- What kind of climate does it have?
- How far is it from the equator?
- Does the country have many mountains?
- Does it have volcanoes?
- Does it have rain forests, deserts, grasslands, or all these habitats?
- What are its biggest cities?
- What special animals live there?

Two of these animals live in rain forests in Brazil. The others live in different habitats, countries, and continents. Find out where each one lives.

lion cub

Amazon parrot

prairie dog

orangutan

15

Who lives there?

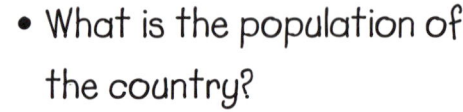

The most important part of a country is its people. The population of some countries, such as Japan, is made up mainly of people whose **ancestors** also lived there for thousands of years. In other countries, such as Canada and the United States, the population is more **diverse**. People from many countries have **immigrated** there. To immigrate is to come to live in a new country.

- What is the population of the country?
- What languages are spoken?
- Does the country have people of many cultures living there?
- What foods, clothing, art, music, and festivals does the country celebrate?
- How does the country's flag look? What do the symbols on the flag stand for?

Australia

United States

Canada

16

 Japan
 Russia
 Indonesia 
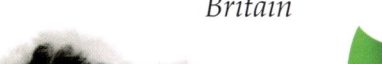 Great Britain
 India 
 Brazil 
 Mexico

Will you write about the people and culture of Indonesia?

What is its history and government?

Countries have histories, or stories about the past.

- Who were the first people who lived in the country?
- How did the land become a country?
- What kind of government does it have?
- Is the leader a king or queen?
- Is the leader a president or prime minister?

Starting your book

Before you start writing, you need to choose which country you want to write about. If you feel happy and excited thinking about your book, you know you have chosen the right country. Read the questions below and write your answers and thoughts in a "writer's notebook" that you will use to record the facts and information about your country.

Should I write about the country where my parents were born?

Questions to ask myself

- Which country will I write about?
- How will I present the information?
- What do I know about a country that I could teach others?
- What interests me the most about my country and other countries?
- Will I write about the country where my parents were born?
- Which country would I like to visit? What would I do there? Would I ski, go snorkeling, or tour a big city?
- How can I make my book about a country exciting to read?
- How will I collect all the information I need?

How will I write this book?

- Will I choose one country and write about it in a lot of detail?
- Will I write about countries on one continent, such as North America, and compare the lands, people, and histories?
- If I write an ABC book, which country or topic will I choose for each letter?
- Should I work with other students so we can share ideas and information? How will we divide the work?

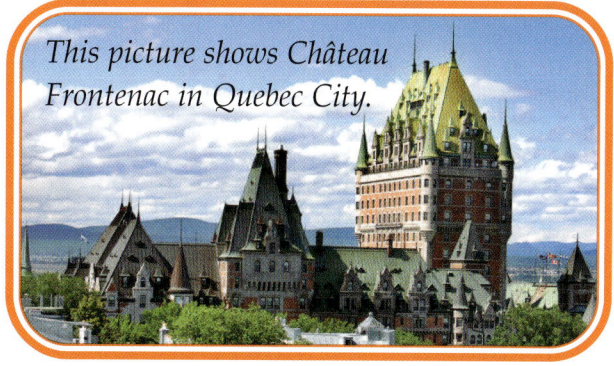

This picture shows Château Frontenac in Quebec City.

Write about the early histories of Canada, the United States, and Mexico and the first people who came to live in each. Which main languages are spoken in each country? What is the official language of the Province of Quebec in Canada?

19

Finding information

There is some information about countries in this book, but you will need to **research**, or look for, more facts for your book. Your school or public library might have some of the country books shown on page 31. These books will give you a great start on your research. You can also find information in other books, encyclopedias, television programs, and on the Internet. While researching, use at least two sources. Take notes, but be sure not to copy someone else's work word for word. Read and understand the information and then rewrite it in your own words.

You can research some of the information you need on the Internet.

Your school library may have all the books you need. If not, you can find many more books at the public library in your community.

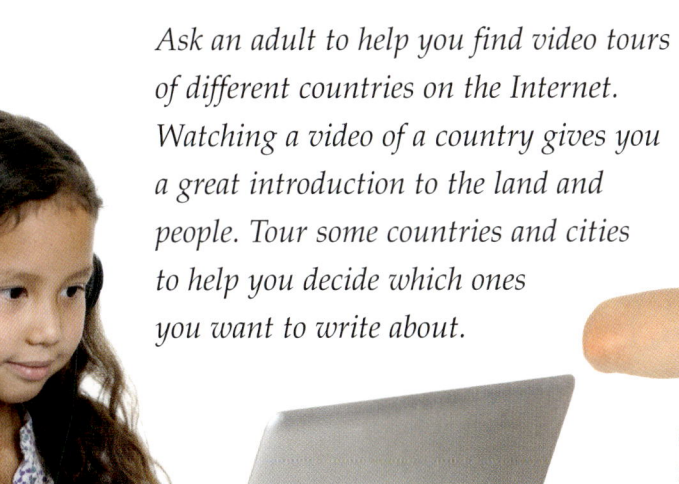

Ask an adult to help you find video tours of different countries on the Internet. Watching a video of a country gives you a great introduction to the land and people. Tour some countries and cities to help you decide which ones you want to write about.

Research review
- Use at least two research sources.
- Write research information in your own words.
- Include your own experiences and photographs of countries you or your family have visited.
- Write stories about the people you met.

The girl on the left was born in Mexico but lives in another country now. She and her family took a vacation there and visited the village where their Mayan ancestors once lived. Ancestors are family members who lived long ago. The girl and her friend are excited to learn about Mexico's history. Would you like to write a book about the country where you, your parents, or your ancestors lived?

If you are doing a book about the country where you live, take photos of important places near your home.

Body of the book

Now that you have decided what kind of book you are writing and done some research, it is time to start writing the **body** of the book. The body of the book will contain the information you have learned and want to share with others.

Chapters, paragraphs, headings

You will find writing a book easier if you organize your ideas into chapters with **headings**. A heading tells you what a chapter is about. A chapter usually has several paragraphs, each with a **subheading**. A subheading is smaller than a chapter heading. It tells you what a paragraph is about. What is the heading of this chapter? What are the subheadings on these two pages?

Bobbie's tip

I have written many books about countries. In each book, I cover one topic in a short chapter called a **spread**. A spread is two pages that face each other. When you write about a topic this way, your information, ideas, and pictures are much easier to organize. This book has 14 spreads. How many spreads will your book have?

Prewriting

- Choose a country that is interesting to you and learn everything about it.
- Make an outline of all the information you want to include. Your outline will become your table of contents.
- Write chapter headings you might use.
- **Interview** people who have lived in the country you are writing about.

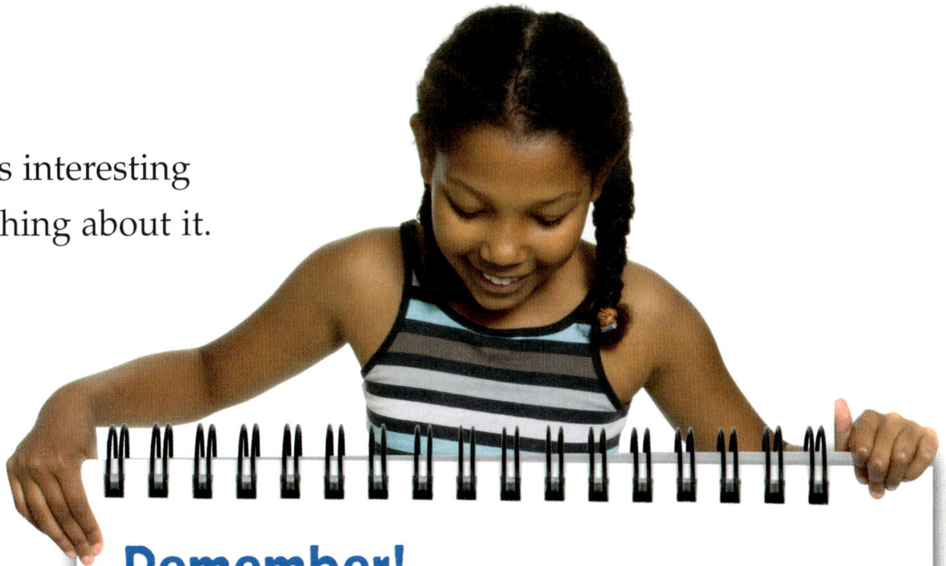

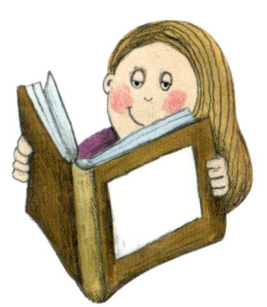

Remember!

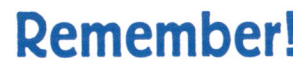

- Write about a country you would like to visit.
- Write down ways to make your book fun, such as using art, activities, and photos.
- Write some ideas for chapter headings.
- Ask people who have lived in other countries to compare their new lives to their lives in their native countries. What do they like the most about their new homes? What do they like the least? What do they miss the most?

Country outline

Welcome to (name of country)!
Where in the world? (maps)
Flags and symbols
Oceans and land
Country life
Big cities
Yesterday and today
(history and government)
Who are the people?
What is the country's culture?
Plants and animals
Activity about the country

Native nations

The first people to live in Canada were native peoples. Hundreds of native **nations**, or groups, lived across North America for thousands of years. Each nation had its own language, leaders, and way of life. Some nations were farmers. They grew corn and other foods. Many also hunted animals and caught food in Canada's oceans, rivers, and lakes.

Some native nations grew corn, beans, and squash. These plants grew well together. Some nations called the plants the "three sisters."

Nations that lived near forests found plenty of animals to hunt, such as turkeys, beavers, and deer.

14

*The Inuit made stone statues called **inukshuks**. Inukshuks showed where people had been. They helped guide travelers across the snowy land.*

Native people, called Inuit, lived in the Arctic. They hunted seals and whales for food. They used sealskins to make warm clothing.

*The Haida lived on Canada's northwest coast. They used cedar trees to make homes and to carve beautiful **totem poles**. Totem poles are tall wooden sculptures. The Haida also built big boats called **canoes**. Some of the canoes could carry many people and goods.*

The Haida made beautiful works of art, such as this cedar box.

15

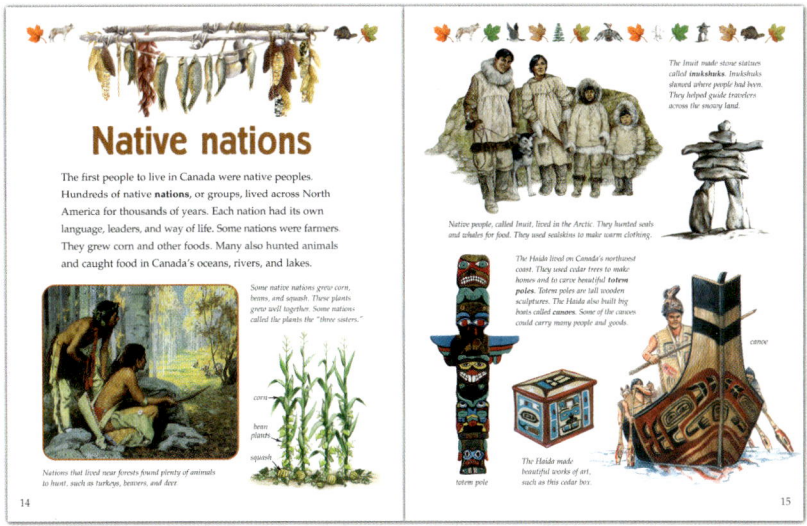

*The picture above shows a spread about some of the native **nations**, or groups, who lived in North America. This spread is from the book* Spotlight on Canada, *shown on page 31.*

Fonts or written words?

You can write your book in different ways. If you are using a computer, you have many type choices. If you are writing your book by hand, you can use colors and different ways of writing that look like typed words on a computer.

What is a font?

A **font** is a style of type. **Plain text** font is the font used for the body of this book. For special features in the book, other kinds of fonts are also used. **Boldface** is a thick black font used for words that may be new to you. Sometimes these words are explained where they appear in the book, and sometimes they are defined in the glossary. The headings and subheadings stand out from the rest of the text by being in a different font, in larger sizes, and in color. For your heading fonts, choose colors that match the pictures on the pages.

What are captions?

The text that gives you information about a picture is called a **caption**. The captions in this book are written in *italics*. Letters in italics slant to the right and are smaller than plain text. **Fact boxes** bring attention to special information, ask questions, or give instructions. There are several fact boxes in this book. They are shown inside pictures that look like notebook pages.

Choosing fonts
- If you are typing your book on a computer, try using some different fonts.
- Choose a plain text font that is easy to read.
- Choose heading fonts that suit your subject.
- If you are writing your book by hand, make words look like **boldface** by using a thick pencil or marker.
- Write captions by *slanting* your words to look like an *italic* font.
- For headings, use markers or colored pencils.

Practice caption writing

Write captions for the pictures on this page. The girl below is beside the Leaning Tower of Pisa, in Italy. Can she keep it from falling? The girl in the bottom picture is in a field in Russia. How do the flowers around her smell? How does the butterfly feel on her skin?

Font review

Plain text font is used to write most of the information in the book.

Boldface font is used to introduce new words.

Italic font is used for writing captions. A caption tells what is happening in a picture.

This font is used in fact boxes that give you extra information or special directions.

Chapter headings are in large colored type.

Subheadings are also in color, but they are smaller than chapter headings.

Revising and editing

Once you have written your **draft**, or first try at writing your book, it is time to read it to yourself. While reading, ask yourself these questions:

- Have I included all the information I wanted to include?
- Have I repeated any information?
- Have I included my own observations or experiences about the country?
- Do my captions give interesting information? Do they describe what is happening in the pictures?
- Do my sentences make sense? Are they in the right order?
- Did I use **comparisons**?
- Have I asked questions to make my readers think?
- How can I **revise**, or rewrite, my book to make it better?

Ask a parent, teacher, or older brother or sister to look at your work and help you organize or improve it. Make the changes you need to make and then share your writing with others.

Share your draft

- After you have read your draft and made some changes, it is time to share it with others.
- What questions did your friends ask? Which parts did they feel needed to be changed?
- Other students can now take turns reading their drafts and asking for suggestions.
- Each person can then rewrite parts of their books that need to be changed.
- Don't worry about making mistakes. Every author revises their book many times!

Editing checklist

Editing is making sure your writing is clear and correct.
- Have you checked your facts?
- Is important information missing?
- Did you use interesting words?
- Do your headings describe the information in your spreads?
- Have you included maps?

Proofreading checklist

Proofreading is checking for errors, such as spelling mistakes, capital letters, and **punctuation**.
- Are your sentences complete?
- Have you used the correct punctuation and capitals?
- Have you spelled names and other words correctly?

*If you are not sure if you have used the right word or spelled it correctly, look it up in a dictionary. To find new and more interesting words to use, look in a **thesaurus**, which contains **synonyms**, or words with the same meanings.*

Questions, questions

There are many questions in this book. Some are questions you ask yourself, and others are asked by others. How does asking questions help you?
- Questions tell you what you have not explained clearly.
- Questions help you review the work you have done and think about what you still need to do.
- They help you think of other ideas to include in your book.
- When you interview other people, or ask them questions, you may learn new information about countries that you could not find in books.

Designing your book

A **design** is a plan that lays out how something will look. Designing your book will make it look good and will help you present your information more clearly. Writing text in a certain way, such as in fact boxes, is part of design. The other very important part includes **visuals**, or different kinds of pictures. Some visuals, such as maps, help your reader see where places are located. Here are some ways to find or create visuals for your book.

Draw and label maps

Maps will help your reader understand where the country, city, or region that you are writing about is located. Picture maps, like the one above right, are fun to draw. Don't forget to include captions.

Photos, maps, artwork

Ask a parent or teacher to show you how to find pictures to download from the Internet. Do a search of the kinds of maps, photographs, or artwork you need. Many photographs and works of art can be downloaded for free. Include the sources of your pictures on your copyright page. Ask your family and friends if they have pictures to lend you for your book. You can also draw or paint your own pictures.

This picture map shows where animals live in Africa. What kind of picture map could you draw to give visual information about your country?

Paint pictures of the country you are writing about. This picture shows how people around the world can live together in peace. How do you feel about world peace? Show it in a painting or write a poem about your feelings.

Finishing up

Publishing your book is the last step. If you did your book on the computer, you could make an eBook that many students could enjoy. Before you publish your book on the computer or by hand, you will need to complete all the parts of the book you learned about on pages 6 and 7: the copyright page; table of contents; glossary; and index. Find these pages in this book and use them to make your own pages.

Glossary

Make a picture dictionary or word glossary and put it at the end of your book. Define special words about countries that your readers may not know. Sort the glossary in alphabetical order.

Index

The index is a list of topics readers look for in a book. It is in alphabetical order and gives the page numbers of where the topics can be found (see page 32).

Copyright page

Your copyright page will include the names of all the people who helped you with your book: parents, friends, teachers, as well as sources of your art and photos. This page may also have a dedication. To whom will you dedicate your book?

Table of contents

Your table of contents is a list of the headings of all the spreads you wrote. The page numbers can be placed at the left or right of the headings. (See page 3.)

Cover and title page

You need to design an attractive cover and title page for your book. After you have completed these, ask your teacher or librarian to help you publish your book so others can read it. One easy way to protect your book is to place the pages in a folder with plastic page protectors. If you photocopy your pages before you slide them into the page protectors, you will have your original copy from which you can make more books. Binders often have plastic pockets on the front and back, as well. You can slide your cover pictures into those. The spine will also have a thin plastic pocket for your title. Below is a sample front and back cover with a spine. Above right is a title page.

title page

binders with plastic pages

back cover　　　　　*front cover*

Bobbie's country books

On this page are a few of the many books I have written about countries. Find them in your library. They will help you write your book about countries.

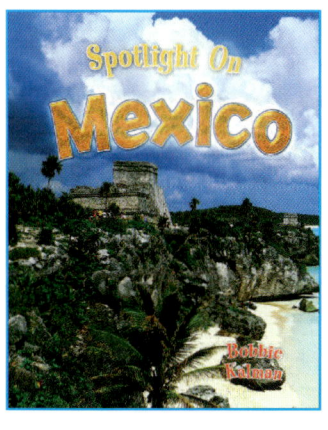
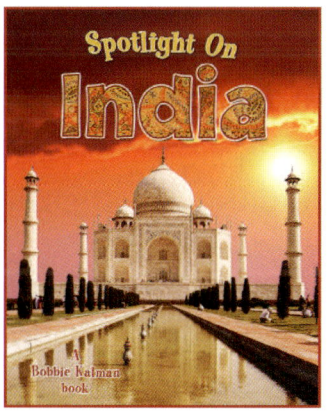
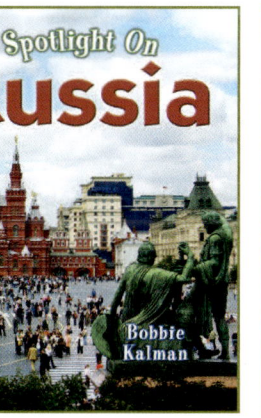
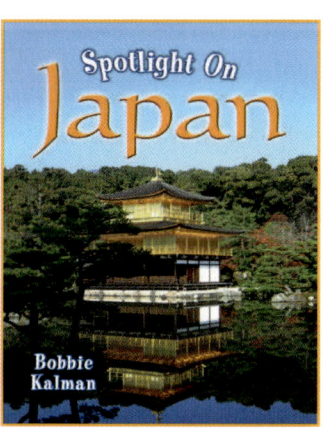

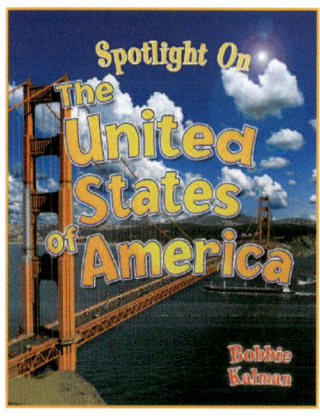

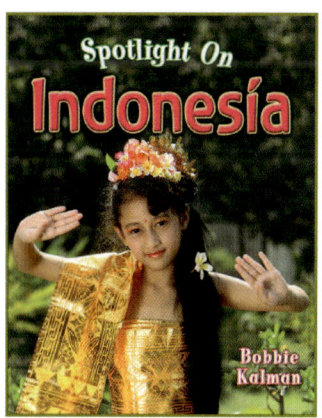

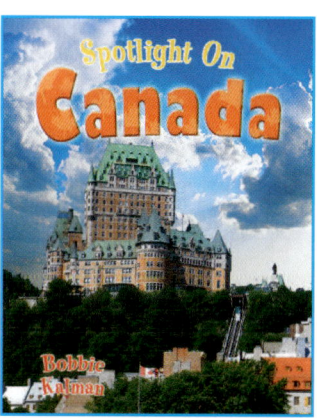
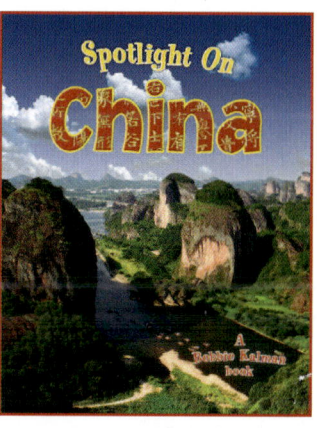
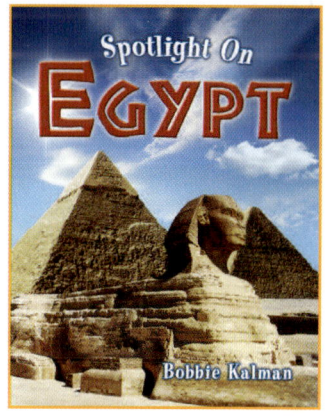

Glossary

Note: Some boldfaced words are defined where they appear in the book.
caption A description about a picture
comparison The act of determining the likenesses and differences in a situation, object, or event
diverse Describing a great deal of variety in people or things
draft A first version or rough copy of written material, such as a book
editing Reading, checking facts, and revising parts of someone's writing
generation A group of people born around the same time and who come from a common ancestor
proofreading Checking a book for spelling, grammar, and punctuation
publisher A person or company that is responsible for printing and distributing a written book
punctuation The use of marks, such as periods or commas, to make the meaning of a sentence clear
representative A person chosen by the people of a country to speak for them and address their needs
revise To correct something or rewrite it to make it better
spread Two pages of a book that face each other
visuals Different kinds of pictures, such as maps, photographs, and artwork, used in illustrating facts and designing a book

Index

body of book 22–23, 24
captions 24, 25, 26
chapters 7, 22
climate 8, 14, 15
copyright 7, 28, 29
continents 9, 12, 15, 19
cover 6, 30
cultures 5, 9, 14, 16, 17, 23
design 28–29, 30
editing 26, 27
fact boxes 24, 25, 28
fonts 24–25
glossary 7, 8, 24, 29
government 8, 14, 17, 23
headings 22, 23, 24, 25, 27, 29
index 7, 29
landforms 10, 14
languages 5, 9, 10, 16, 19
maps 12–13, 27, 28
outline 23
pictures 6, 19, 21, 22, 23, 24, 25, 26, 28, 29
publishing 4, 29, 30
questions 15, 18, 24, 26, 27
research 20–21, 22
spreads 22, 23, 29
table of contents 7, 23, 29
title page 7, 30
writer's notebook 13, 18